With Signs Following

David Ricks's poems have appeared in American magazines over the last three decades; a pamphlet of them, *Shreds and Patches*, was published by Rack Press in 2022. He has written about many of the modern Greek poets who matter and has published versions from the work of some.

With Signs Following

David Ricks

Also by Two Rivers Poets

David Attwooll, *The Sound Ladder* (2015)
Charles Baudelaire, *Paris Scenes* translated by Ian Brinton (2021)
William Bedford, *The Dancers of Colbek* (2020)
Kate Behrens, *Man with Bombe Alaska* (2016)
Kate Behrens, *Penumbra* (2019)
Kate Behrens, *Transitional Spaces* (2022)
Conor Carville, *English Martyrs* (2019)
David Cooke, *A Murmuration* (2015)
David Cooke, *Sicilian Elephants* (2021)
Tim Dooley, *Discoveries* (2022)
Jane Draycott, *Tideway* (re-issued 2022)
Jane Draycott & Lesley Saunders, *Christina the Astonishing* (re-issued 2022)
Claire Dyer, *Yield* (2021)
Claire Dyer, *The Adjustments* (2024)
John Froy, *Sandpaper & Seahorses* (2018)
John Froy, *The Blue Armchair* (2024)
James Harpur, *The Examined Life* (2021)
Maria Teresa Horta, *Point of Honour* translated by Lesley Saunders (2019)
Ian House, *Just a Moment* (2020)
Philippe Jaccottet, *In Winter Light* translated by Tim Dooley (2022)
Rosie Jackson, *Love Leans over the Table* (2023)
Rosie Jackson & Graham Burchell, *Two Girls and a Beehive: Poems about Stanley Spencer and Hilda Carline* (2020)
Martha Kapos, *Music, Awake Her* (2024)
Gill Learner, *Chill Factor* (2016)
Gill Learner, *Change* (2021)
Sue Leigh, *Chosen Hill* (2018)
Sue Leigh, *Her Orchards* (2021)
Becci Louise, *Octopus Medicine* (2017)
Mairi MacInnes, *Amazing Memories of Childhood, etc.* (2016)
Steven Matthews, *On Magnetism* (2017)
Steven Matthews, *Some Other Where* (2023)
Katherine Meehan, *Dame Julie Andrews' Botched Vocal Cord Surgery and Other Poems* (2023)
Henri Michaux, *Storms under the Skin* translated by Jane Draycott (2017)
Kate Noakes, *Goldhawk Road* (2023)

Alistair Noon, *Paradise Takeaway* (2023)
René Noyau, *Earth on Fire and other Poems* translated by Gérard Noyau with Peter Pegnall (2021)
Ruth O'Callaghan, *Where Shadow Falls* (2023)
James Peake, *Reaction Time of Glass* (2019)
James Peake, *The Star in the Branches* (2022)
Peter Robinson & David Inshaw, *Bonjour Mr Inshaw* (2020)
Peter Robinson, *English Nettles* (re-issued 2022)
Peter Robinson, *Retrieved Attachments* (2023)
Lesley Saunders, *Nominy-Dominy* (2018)
Lesley Saunders, *This Thing of Blood & Love* (2022)
Jack Thacker, *Handling* (2018)
Robin Thomas, *The Weather on the Moon* (2022)
Susan Utting, *The Colour of Rain* (2024)
Jean Watkins, *Precarious Lives* (2018)

First published in the UK in 2024 by Two Rivers Press
7 Denmark Road, Reading RG1 5PA.
www.tworiverspress.com

© David Ricks 2024

The right of the poet to be identified as the author of this work has been asserted by him in accordance with the Copyright, Designs and Patents Act of 1988.

All rights reserved. No part of this publication may be reproduced, stored in or introduced into a retrieval system, or transmitted, in any form, or by any means (electronic, mechanical, photocopying, recording or otherwise) without the prior written permission of the publisher.

ISBN 978-1-915048-19-6

1 2 3 4 5 6 7 8 9

Two Rivers Press is represented in the UK by Inpress Ltd and distributed by BookSource, Glasgow

Cover design by Sally Castle
Text design by Nadja Guggi and typeset in Janson and Parisine

Printed and bound in Great Britain by CMP (UK), Poole

Acknowledgements

The following poems, sometimes in earlier versions, first appeared elsewhere:

- 'Tower-Houses, Southern Peloponnese' in *Atlanta Review*
- 'A White Officer in 1945', 'In Darkness Let Him Dwell', 'A Photograph from 1963', and 'The Sadducees' in *Drastic Measures*
- 'The Full Professors' in *The Epigrammatist*
- 'A Televised Bullfight' in *The Florida Review*
- 'Prelude' in *The Formalist*
- 'Homeward, Late...' and 'The Ships' in *Kondylophoros*
- 'Jack in the Box', 'Mr Eliot's Confession', 'The Euthanasiast', and 'To Louis Aragon Et Al.' in *Literary Imagination*
- 'Solitude' in Joanna Kruczkowska (ed.), *Landscapes of Irish and Greek Poets* (Peter Lang, 2018)
- 'Après le déluge', 'Marche funèbre et perpendiculaire', and 'Sculptor from Tyana' in *Modern Poetry in Translation*
- 'Among the Volga Rus, AD 921' and 'Second-Hand' in *New England Review*
- 'The Studio' and 'Vacuum' in *Pivot*
- 'The Character of the Country' in *Poem*
- 'Cantata for Anton Webern', 'Cavafy's Stationery', '"Ethnic Cleansing"', 'Genius Loci', 'Shreds and Patches', 'After Ruisdael', and 'Variation on a Theme of Baudelaire' in *Poetry* (the last poem also in *The Poetry Anthology, 1912–2002*)
- 'A Sketch from the Levant', 'Cycladic', and 'For William Lawes' in *Southern Humanities Review*
- 'A Veteran of the Terror', 'Incident', 'Still-Life with Musical Instruments', and 'With Signs Following' in *Southwest Review*
- 'Cycladic' first appeared on a card, *Diptych* (Cloisters Press, 1992). Ten of the poems were first collected in the pamphlet *Shreds and Patches* (Rack Press, 2022), for which thanks are due to Nicholas Murray.

Contents

Prelude | xiv

I.

A Televised Bullfight | 2
Incident | 3
Jack in the Box | 4
Among the Volga Rus, AD 921 | 5
Second-Hand | 6
Untitled | 7
The Euthanasiast | 8
'Ethnic Cleansing' | 9
To Louis Aragon Et Al. | 10
A White Officer in 1945 | 11
A Veteran of the Terror | 12
XX | 13

II.

Angleton's Names | 16

III.

With Signs Following | 24
The Sadducees | 25
The Full Professors | 26
Vacuum | 27
Shreds and Patches | 28

IV.

Solitude (*Kostis Palamas*) | 30
Homeward, Late... (*Tellos Agras*) | 31
Sculptor from Tyana (*C. P. Cavafy*) | 32
Cavafy's Stationery | 33
Marche funèbre et perpendiculaire (*after K. G. Karyotakis*) | 34
Fecit | 35
Line Numberings | 36

V.

Foscolo in London: Five Acts | 38

VI.

Homage to Johannes Bobrowski | 44
Cantata for Anton Webern | 45
For William Lawes | 46
In Darkness Let Him Dwell | 47
Genius Loci | 48
The Ships (*Konstantinos Chatzopoulos*) | 49

VII.

The Studio | 52
A Sketch from the Levant | 54
Postcard | 55
Variation on a Theme of Baudelaire | 56
Still-Life with Musical Instruments | 57
After Ruisdael | 58
Landscape, with Crumbling Wall | 59
The Angelus | 60
A Photograph from 1963 | 61
The Character of the Country | 62

VIII.

Unpainted Pictures | 64

IX.

Mr Eliot's Confession | 70
Mackonochie Chapel | 71
Tower-Houses, Southern Peloponnese | 72
Après le déluge (*Nasos Vayenas*) | 73
Cycladic | 74

Notes | 76
Afterword, by A. E. Stallings | 78

In memory of Dhiren Bhagat

Prelude

Speak softly when you near a mass of snow:
A raised voice can bring on an avalanche.
The guide who says so is the one to know:

He's seen a morning skier's laughter launch
A weight of snow that's waited up all night
Just for the fun of seeing a skier blanch.

His imminent erasure by the white
Lends his skis wings, his voice a higher pitch;
The skein of his last cry, as he takes flight,

Extends behind him like a bright scarf which
No-one will see, to mark its resting place,
Except the guide, high up and out of reach,

Blank silence spreading over the mountain face.

I.

A Televised Bullfight

Watch Juan Antonio Ruiz Espartaco
Take centre stage, as dainty as a doll,
The swirling passes of his cape now rousing
Cheers or a few wild bars from the brass band.
As in some simile, the bull is felled.
The whole thing has a certain artistry.

It could be said that these things often do.
Admonitory, stepping from his canvas
In the museum into this hotel room
In sleep's place, here comes Saint Bartholomew
Holding a knife and – draped over one arm
Casually, like a pale cape – his own skin.

Incident

Over to Ulster, and a place called Darkley.
'Meeting house', a sober enough name,
Seems rather grand used of this shack
Whose cousins sprouted in the Appalachians,
Where you may come upon a large sign who
Knows who has planted, stating
Improbably, yet all but irresistibly:
JESUS IS COMING.

Before this tabernacle Pastor Robert Bain,
Through teeth unflattered by the camera's attentions,
Relates, with frontier stoicism
Or in plain shock, what came to pass.
The sound team splices in corroboration:

Whether by custom or by premonition,
The worshippers had a tape recorder running.
At the verse, *Are ye washed in the blood of the Lamb?*
We hear the sound of automatic fire.

Jack in the Box

Co. Armagh, 1997

The shops are kindly
Requested to close
As a mark of respect,

And sad captains
Have hooded their heads
To pose with their pistols:

FORCE LEAD THE WAY
The draped banner's injunction
Or terse misspelt tale

As they move to a skirl
Of pipes through a town
Which tenses itself

For the music to stop
For the *lex talionis*
Of Jack in the box.

Among the Volga Rus, AD 921

The Caliph's emissary had been anxious
To see a heathen cremation ceremony.
His lawyerly account sticks to the facts.

'Which of you will die with him?' was the question.
The answer 'I!' could never be taken back.
That girl's last days were spent drinking and singing.

He reached the river and there he saw the boat.
They were saying something he couldn't understand
About an old woman they called the angel of death.

The corpse was propped on cushions in the vessel,
Liquor and fruit and a lute laid out beside him
To lend his final voyage music and savour.

The girl was going up and down from one
Tent to another. One man after another
Went with her. Gladly she lent herself.

She could see her master seated in Paradise
And Paradise was green and fair. She took
Both of her bracelets off, both of her anklets.

She sang and drank and said all her farewells
Until they led her bewildered to the tent
On the funeral boat. Then shields were beaten with sticks.

Six men entered the tent and had their way.
Then as two of them tugged at her feet and two at her hands
And two hauled at the noose around her neck,

The angel thrust the knife between her ribs
In and out, in one place after another.
And then the blaze, fanned by great gales of laughter.

Second-Hand

And here's *Mein Kampf* in English, leather-
Bound, with the inscription *1939*.
A gift from one person to another,
The donor prudent enough not to sign

His name in full: it just says *M*.
Guilty perhaps of stereotyping,
I take it instinctively for a man's name
And the gift as made to a woman. The whole thing

At this distance hard to decipher.
Does the date show him confident,
Or is it a fact like the weather?
Is *M* code or the mere abbreviation of a confidant?

And what of the rest of the story?
Does M repent, like many?
Or does he end up like John Amery
On the wrong side, hanged on the fall of Germany?

M and friend in 1939.
The outcome for them we pick
Depends on a reading of that title-page's sign:
'From Sanskrit *svasti*, "well-being, fortune, luck".'

Untitled

By way of street or beetling alley, they left. Here, a calvary stands (stood?) as a warning; there a plaque admonishes, to what avail. Sometimes, it was a knoll that marked their passing, sometimes a marsh, freezing or thawing, who can tell. A grassed-over path between dark pines; a close copse of half-timbered houses, black and white. Crows flying ahead, vans nosing blunt over cobbles, a tree now struggling into leaf. Over hillocks, crossing stone or sand, by field and fen; along a shaded path, through glades, to their long home.

The Euthanasiast

1941

Emil's cards from hospital: 'Happy Easter!',
This one says brightly, in a nurse's hand.

He drew a rabbit, eggs, and a fat spring cloud
Which in a telegram the following winter

Had darkened and blown away to the far north-east
In the form of a frank. EMIL·DIED·SUDDENLY

While, in some lecture room's sunshine of theory,
Unclouded, Dr N. warmed to his theme.

'Ethnic Cleansing'

The arguments remained specious.
Meanwhile things followed the atrocious

Imperative. The century
Had done away with sanctuary.

Populations fell into the chasm
Opened by each neologism.

To Louis Aragon Et Al.

In each of your Party
Lines a caesura
Clove a head from a body:
You marshalled ruthless feet.

Till we made out your syntax
We couldn't see how cunning
A hyperbaton separated the 'who'
From the 'whom'.

Then the ear became attuned
To the assonance of one body
Dropping after another

Into lime.
With each enjambment we could hear a man
Torn limb from limb.

A White Officer in 1945

Long lines of cavalry bestrew the past
As he surveys it, pacing up and down
His one room, far from Russia. With a frown
He gives Kolchak and Wrangel each one last
Chance. (That Denikin proved to be a clown!)
How could he never have foreseen how fast
That check would come which took away the crown?
His heart's flag permanently at half-mast.

On days like this he always finds he needs
(More than the drink, which only makes him sad)
The thought of Russians who preserved the flame:
Those starving botanists of Leningrad
(Though he can't bear to call it by that name)
Who would not eat their inventoried seeds.

A Veteran of the Terror

Sanguinary, but no longer sanguine.
(The great days long gone.) In the forest, pelted.
Some nights near freeze your blood.

Having arrested André Chénier doesn't mean much to you.
In the woods by the Yonne the nymphs
Were forced with dirty smocks, and fauns took casual aim.

The oak-trunks rolled toward Paris,
And you with them. In every tavern, a girl, a quarrel.
And then, in season, the deciduous heads.

Till the reversal. Your old neighbours would have done well
To shoot you dead; and you did well to let them try,
Standing there blasted, waving your valid arm.

Your letters to the courts seeking redress
(Redress – you!) blow in, wildly misspelt,
And are then swept neatly into the archive.

The village boys torment you, out of gunshot range,
As you die slowly rooted in your bed-midden,
Unexpectedly many rings in your hard wood.

XX

Their names make up a menagerie
Or even a cosmology: with Olympian
Detachment, the chair-borne in London
Rule that one come into being,
Another be crossed off. (The Executions
Committee meets rarely, and of course with reluctance.)

Think of Snow and Biscuit in the fog, crossing
The North Sea in a blacked-out trawler,
Each convinced, and rightly, albeit for the wrong
Reasons, that the other is not what he seems.
(Biscuit the survivor, the hardened recidivist;
Snow at length melting away in drink and suspicions.)

Or think of Garbo, alone in Madrid, with just a *Guide Bleu*
And an out-of-date *Bradshaw*, surrounded
By a whole team of fictional helpers.
Eight hours a day at his desk, his style
Luxuriant, even lurid; decorated
By both sides: M.B.E., Iron Cross.

Let us not forget what we owe the duplicitous,
Those of cross purposes, impeachable motives,
Livers on the nerves, drivers of the hard bargain,
Closeted always in a meeting of ends
And means, in the hard places where knots
Are never Gordian: the double agents.

II.

Angleton's Names

Mother

If not an under-the-breath
Imprecation, where did that come from?
Of invention, certainly. Mother Goose?

The first letters are those of his favourite
Adopted child, Mossad. (God knows
What Pound would have said

About that.) Near the end, a journalist
Hears him answer the telephone, *he thinks*,
In Hebrew. Certainly, in discreet

Ceremonies, they honour
James Jesus in the mother-
Lode, Jerusalem.

Orchid

It glows like the semi-precious
Stones he polishes out in Tucson.
He even names a couple, one after
His wife – there's classified for you –

And then in time abandons the Virginia greenhouse
To a tinkling of glass, a wilderness of mirrors;
Like the Agency itself, now withered under
A glare of hearings.

Fisherman

The master image:
Alone, casting
On his own sixteen acres, far away.
At the deep pool a fish, or just a shadow, rising.
Calm moments. Counter-

Espionage is the slow 'distillate
Of counter-intelligence'.
What's your poison?
Here in the chilly stream lie buried,
Every few paces, bottles of Jack Daniel's.

Virginia Slim

Tapping it on his knee, the audience warming to him,
The pinstriped shanks involved.
Authoritative still: 'I do not base this
On reading information
Available at the corner drugstore';

Even when saying, under oath:
'I have no satisfactory answer to your question.'
Met at his club, the James Bond theme going round
And round; or muttering in a car
Parked out on Chain Bridge Road.

Cadaver

The lungs now wrecked.
The bearer of Allen Dulles' ashes
Downing the Coca-Colas, yet still angular
As the El Greco

Reproduction in his student room.
In hiding? Nonsense! His name is in the book,
And messages still pile up on (remember them?)
The answering machine.

The Poet

'Gerontion': even for an old man's
Funeral, a rum choice.
The whole thing started, you might say, with a little magazine's
Intentional obscurity. Some habits
Never change: a single lamp

Burning, papers always
Face down. Just once,
A poem of his got clipped in error to a report.
Almost a definition of the poet, this:
'He can remember his own lies.'

III.

With Signs Following

A Photograph from 1969

They pose here, each with a little venomous
Snake in one hand – almost a parody
Of a *Laocoon*; though here an altar
– Or rather, lectern – stands between the two;
Whose orphan-faces seem anonymous,
Drained of some self inside, and blankly ready
– Sons of the Word, they know what they must do –
To test God's love (or: try Ananke's halter).
One wears a curious tunic reading: 'THAy
SHALL TAKE UP SERPENTs' (of the 'deadly thing'
No mention here).
                     – Unlettered literalists,
We know your names, Buford and Jimmy Ray;
We know that, four years hence, a wild faith twists
The life from you, by strychnine poisoning.

The Sadducees

Time's yellow press will, of course, cover them.
Misquoted by the peddlers of good news,
Listed in error with the unbelievers,
They will even come to be diagnosed
As a disease of the heart. Recurrent faddists
Will be inveighing against their silver spoons
And their cholesterol; hands will be wrung
Over the retributions of their Law;
Enthusiasts will find in their denial
Of angels and spirits a want of imagination.
Time's yellow press will of course cover them.

The Full Professors

The brain succumbs at length to tertiary
Literature: we can cite, but we can't see.

Vacuum

And when the little bag
Is emptied of its dust,
One finds a life's detritus
Forming a pattern at last:
Compact and square and grey;
Reconciling
         – it's just
That the glint of a needle's showing
Some opportunity lost.

Shreds and Patches

Clad in the only-once-to-be-unravelled
Accumulations of what must be years
(How long? The crusted face contains no answer)
Out on the streets, this man has piled his layers
Higher than merely bodily warmth requires.
His step perforce slowed, figure now imposing
As Henry VIII with codpiece, he assumes
The furred bulk of some Viking chieftain, say,
Invested king in a half-remembered movie.
His past cohering round his present self
He bears heavily, regally almost,
Proud with accretions bodying out the years.

This is a syndrome no doubt documented
In 'the literature'; a milder form of which
Is found in those who haunt our libraries,
Turning up daily with their great bags full
Of papers, tiny papers, paper empires
Perhaps originating in some dotty
Research (the man who'd patiently inserted
'Roman' each time the book I borrowed had
The word 'Catholic'), yet long turned sibylline:
Warming as down or layers of warm clothes
But breathing as their owners mutter round them
Only a dark afflatus in reply.

IV.

Solitude

Graft of care
Gnawing at me… – away!
In the garden here,
In a reverie.

   Here a haven.
None to intrude.
Seek not to leaven
My solitude.

   Nor am I – remember –
A bird on the wing
Or a breeze or a leaf…

   Unblossoming,
Somehow I live,
Straight tree, grey timber.

Kostis Palamas

Homeward, Late…

Homeward late as I stray
benighted, I reach the square
with the lonely streetlight hanging,
a damp night wind blowing there
fit to shake it from its string
and tug it away.

This muffled wind's just right
for the skittish light
that trembles against the walls,
for the knots of small prodigals
now left to themselves in the gloom,
not a soul to call them home.

And the kites snagged in the wires
and the windows' flapping papers
– not a mark but has its mate.
And the flat accordion
weeping who knows where – and late,
at some dingy junction,

seems one with my shadow (passing
on, veering off to the corner;
at which point a wind whisks it away
like the sad chestnut-tree
plucked bare by the winter weather),
seems one with my shadow passing.

Tellos Agras

Sculptor from Tyana

You'll have heard I'm no tyro.
I see my share of stone.
Back home, in Tyana, I'm quite well known.
And here too I've had a good many statues
commissioned by senators.
                              And let me show you
a few without further ado. Notice that Rhea:
august, primordial, austere.
Notice that Pompey. Marius,
Aemilius Paullus, Scipio Africanus.
To the best of my abilities, true copies.
Patroclus (I shall be touching him up a little later on).
There, by those bits of yellow
marble, is Caesarion.

And lately I've been taken up for quite some time
with the making of a Neptune. My concern
is above all his horses, how to shape them.
They must be light as if
their bodies and their feet are visibly
not treading earth but racing over the sea.

But here's the piece dearest of all to me,
on which I worked with feeling and with the greatest care;
this one here, on a hot summer's day,
my mind ascending to the realm of the ideal,
this one here in my dreams, young Mercury.

C. P. Cavafy

Cavafy's Stationery

Accustomed as he was to holding things
Up to the light to see what others missed,
Did he ever peruse these watermarks?
Did Conqueror London set him musing on empires
Once crescent, or Old Hickory evoke
A new world growing into history?
And did he start to dream of warriors
Combing their hair, of their deep sense of duty
– Not *so* unlike his to his craft and city –
Each time his pencil marked the Spartan Bond?

Marche funèbre et perpendiculaire

I gaze at the plaster ceiling.
The meander's dance starts to attract.
Happiness, I reflect,
must be somehow uplifting.

Artifice of eternity,
roses without end,
thorns in a white garland,
a great horn of plenty.

(Art degree zero,
how late I come round to your point!)
Dream relief, I shall make your ascent
like some alpinist hero.

Horizons of expectations
would only close in on me later:
life's stale bread and butter,
the affairs, the frustrations.

Yes, that nice plaster crown –
time for its unveiling.
framed by the ceiling,
how well I'll go down!

after K. G. Karyotakis

Fecit

How like you in that first
Poem to find a place
For your name in the unobtrusive
Form of an adjective
In lower case,
Yet with the pride
Of a small-town alderman
Laying the parish hall's first brick.

From 'Domicilium', you stuck
To the plan you'd begun:
Foundations laid,
And then the house
Fit for your words to live
In long after your elusive
Ghost had flown. And the verse,
Hardy, you knew would last.

Line Numberings

We knew for certain the poet had died
When in the first posthumous edition
Figures crept for the first time
Along the page's edge
Irrefutable unwelcome
The traces of death indelible
From page to page to page
His death that is or even the dying
Of the life in each line
As the fresh glance had scanned it
Making all the connections for itself
Two voices meeting unobserved

V.

Foscolo in London: Five Acts

I. Holland House

A hero's welcome!
Lionized. Life

And soul of a party.
His galloping broken

English strikes
A chord in fair bosoms.

No need for
Buskin where fierce

Whiskers bristle and a revolutionist's
Blouse falls open

As if to receive
The fatal blow.

II. Digamma Cottage

Not far
From Little Venice
Otium
Enthusiasm diminished
To a conceit

Just as
Tombs had once drawn
Him with a mind to
Horse-taming Hector
And his monument

So here he seized
On a lost letter
Posting it
At his door:
A slanted *F*.

III. Somers Town

Conveyed to Chalton Street
The three maids gone
And one
With child (not his).

In better days
Known as
Le Grazie. Apple
Of discord, more like!

The epic quarrels
Over some slattern
In the street outside
Nagging away at him

As, chafing,
He spurs himself
Once more to Greek
And Homer.

IV. Turnham Green

The battle lost.
The corse now tied
To its cart of debt.

V. Chiswick

Entombed, courtesy of the Church
By law established:

'Wearied Citizen Poet'
The legend;

The remains long since
Translated.

Content now? Not
An earthly.

Ever-restless
Wandering half-Greek.

VI.

Homage to Johannes Bobrowski

Clavichord
Barely heard
From the next room

Lebensraum
Of the dead

Out of time

Cantata for Anton Webern

It begins
Like the report
Of a jittery
Sentry's gun
In an occupied zone

Raised voices
Wrung notes
Hardly easy
Listening, everything
Exposed

Matter of minutes
Like a summer
Wind it leaves
Us wondering
How it begins

For William Lawes

Master of discords, did your keen nerves sense
The march of armies, or that you would fall
('Betrayed thereunto by adventurousness')
At Chester in the King's name – interval
Not even you could span – and leave old scores
(Your wounds unsalved, for all your viols' skill)
To bring the long-awaited resolution?

In Darkness Let Him Dwell

Dowland in Denmark

More toping and (who knows?) petards tonight.
The tablature abandoned for the table:
The groaning board; the tuneless rattle of dice.
(How quickly virtuoso turns to vice.)

A flourish; drums. His head rings with that babel
(Rhyme him with dole, whose lute's soft notes are drowned)
And his heart grows as fretful as the Sound
When its grey waves are played on by the light.

Genius Loci

In Buxtehude's church in Elsinore
The organ can be heard playing his music
And conjuring into life the whitewashed walls
And patterned pipes and pews of vanished gentry,
And even those in doubt may see the little
Tutelary ship high in the nave
Dance and then settle on a calming sea.

The Ships

And eyes open to the blur
and eyes as if lost in a vision,
and eyes smothered by the blur
look out on the ships afar,
ships as if lost in a vision.
One daybreak they left dry land,
their sails spread like a vision,
and the waters laughed before them
and wings fluttered about them
in the sails they unfurled to the wind.
And the azure was a dream before them
and a white dream they left behind them,
their sails unfurled like a vision,
but far out they were seized by a mist
with sails unfurled it seized them
and they were left with sails unfurled
the ships as if lost in a vision.–
Lost in a foreign daybreak
in a silence all round unstirring
unstirring unfurled as if dead
their sails on the bleared waters
eyes gaze on them from afar
on the ships like dreams long vanished.

Konstantinos Chatzopoulos

VII.

The Studio

The last three years, on reaching
Three score and ten, he stopped
Writing, reading, listening to music.
He gave away his two violins,
And, not without a pang, he let the family
Redecorate the Studio, covering over
The peeling frescoes painted by his friends
Some forty years before. The shelves were dismantled;
Most of the books went to two libraries,
And he went rapidly downhill.

A student of Latin, he must once have prayed,
Like Horace, to be of sound mind at the end
And not without the cithara.
We can't know whether the body or the mind gave out;
And if the mind, whether it did so voluntarily.
An actuary will tell you that conductors
And rabbis are out in front; but he, teacher
And musician, was also of the irritable
Race of poets. Impulsive and pedantic,
He ruined some of his best work with revisions.

He seems to have vowed, like his beloved Rilke,
'To be always beginning, always to be a beginner'.
Hence the false starts:
A poem on astronomy, dabblings
With a new religion, dud dramas,
Vers libre later torn up in disgust.
Of his music, three sonatas are left,
And a song without words.
A phrase from *Tender is the Night* might fit him:
'Fragmentary, suggestive, and surpassed.'

The town is all but unrecognizable
Under the Sixties concrete.
Try to imagine the Studio still there:
The little circle passing round its little magazine;
Rare writings being taken from the shelves
And praised to the accompaniment of preludes and inventions;
And, with the burnished phonograph crackling to life,
Glasses clinking, and the paint moistening
On frescoes and the hands that painted them.

A Sketch from the Levant

And in the hatching of each grimy doorway,
A shade too knobbly-kneed or lantern-jawed,
There they stand curiously
                                  dressed in the black
Of brief and oft-renewed viduity,
Late risers
              among whom a five-o'clock
Shadow steals under rouge
                              with some delay,
But no less calculably than the dunes
Move on, hasteless,
                        lending the desert shapes
That make the waking traveller afraid.

Postcard

That restaurant's plastic chairs
White as sepulchres

And empty; awnings
Furled for the winter; swings

Now still under the willows;
All the pedalos

Up-ended on the shore; and, in the gutter,
Cursory, a French letter.

Variation on a Theme of Baudelaire

On sale at every English station
Bookshop: *Gray's Anatomy*,
Permanently remaindered –
Almost as embarrassing to be
Seen perusing as the configuration
Of bodies on a king-size bed

On that sex manual's cover: luminous
(Albeit remaindered) forms condemned
To permanent tumescence,
The bones and muscles limned
In *Gray* now seeming so laborious,
Losing the essence

Of those still figures which are full of arrows
Yet suffer nothing,
Wrapped in the decency of polysyllables,
Exempt from all that writhing
With strange flesh on positioned pillows,
Knowing no troubles.

Still-Life with Musical Instruments

The open score
Some kind of overture.

The objects shuffle, arrange
Themselves. An orange

Unpeeled. A violin
Out of its case, one string

Broken. A clarinet's
Open mouth. A spinet

Reticent as a tiny
Coffin. (The unspent money

In that box round which everything
Seems to revolve.) This lute gathering

Dust, dead in its shell.
And a curtain ready to fall.

After Ruisdael

Pictures half-recollected from the mind's
Poorly lit galleries this November evening:

A windmill's sails; clouds pressing on damp thatch;
That low warped hill, those clenched indignant trees;

The women, long uncoifed, making their way,
The thick paint clinging to their pattens.

Landscape with Crumbling Wall

Long sedentary, Caspar David Friedrich
looks into his mind's eye
                                and sees a wall
warm from the sun

                            yet casting a dark shadow
in his direction
                which a half-open gate
breaks

        to reveal a wide and fertile slope
and far away
                – we barely make it out,

the old chorale
                      half-hidden in the parts –
a tiny Dresden rising into spears.

The Angelus

The bell is barely
Made out, like a spire
Across the fields at dusk.
But she knows the time:
Six of the clock,
And their work is done.

He could be holding his hat
A little nervously
As if in courtship,
As if seeking her hand
With feats of the fork
Stuck in the clods beside him.

He could be revolving
His hat with some impatience:
When will she be done?
Her heaped fruitfulness
Comes between them.
She bows beneath its weight.

A Photograph from 1963

Red fire in grey water:
Watch the sea's youngest daughter
      Trip and curtsey,

Raising steamy flounces to the mother
Of old Pangaea. Here's another
      Island: Surtsey!

The Character of the Country

This river holds
The curve of a fly rod
In eddies and smoothnesses
Free of bubbles and fatted weed:

Through the lines
Of Bewick's black and white,
Eyes straining, hearts at ease,
We are coming home.

VIII.

Unpainted Pictures
Emil Nolde, 1941–1945

'Resist', of you,
is a bit much.
Let us say you withstood.

I would resort
to rhyme or something akin
to it to probe

your case, just as you reached
for what colours
were to hand.

We can hardly
take you at your word,
who read just one book (you said)

in your whole life.

The truckling over
at last, you watched, grown truculent,
from that strange

mound-house
in the marshland:
barrow or, better, lump

of oils on the palette.
At water-colours now,
whose scent gives nothing

away. No canvases:
rice-paper you could have
swallowed

if it came to it.

Knowing nothing
of the fate
of the 1052

confiscated paintings,
regenerate,
you committed

yourself to these
as numerous sheets.
Forgive

us if we turn from the
giants and dancing
girls and from anything that even

reminds us of the human

to seek those matted
fields brushed
by sluices

swept by
clouds
washing

the world with colour
that runs
even as we sleep

over black waves
blurred beacon
glowing

sun.

IX.

Mr Eliot's Confession

S. Silas the Martyr, Kentish Town, early 1950s

With the regularity of a distinguished
Quarterly review

An elder statesman peregrinates
To – of all places – this presbytery.

His word here, tendered,
Will not leave these four walls.

The inexplicable
Splendour has come to assume

Explicitness. An interrogatory
Wooden guild of saints

Cluttering an 'odd expressionist
Gothic' of the year of grace 1911

Furnishes its own startling answer:
These bones can live.

Mackonochie Chapel

S. Alban the Martyr, Holborn

Slum priest in your newfangled chasuble,
Teetotallers were Manichees, you preached –
A gospel that endeared you to the people

You ministered to for twenty years with love.
Today, from your richly decorated niche,
Recumbent, it may be that you absolve

Even the fan who's painted ARSENAL –
Witless inebriate tribute to the Church
Militant – on this chapel's outside wall.

Tower-Houses, Southern Peloponnese

A row of them, mouthing imprecations,
Slighted. *Those plagued clans.* Pillars of salt
Painfully gathered. The after-taste.

A concrete path generously endowed
By a widower. The silent new belfry.
Who knows what crosses on what doors.

In a corner, the seated figure of a man
Blowing a policeman's whistle. Again and again.
His patient dog. The old motives –

No impugning them. The aerials' heraldry.
Somewhere, behind closed shutters,
Inextinguishable canned laughter.

Après le déluge

The immortal lips unwiped.
The sun transparent, a cognac bottle dropped

as soon as drained by an abandoned
god. The doves valiantly defend

what of the high places has survived disaster.
Here and there bits of plaster

come down on the heads of the mortals who'd let
raw nature overwhelm old habit.

A peacock walking through the water-spill,
opening wide a shit-bespattered tail.

At the taxi windows a line of whores
chewing gum, tooting the horns.

Jewels gleaming on the fingers of the dark.
The winds returning to their sack.

Nasos Vayenas

Cycladic

With what scholarly warrant
I confess I am ignorant,

The curator has arranged
These familiar, strange

Statuettes in a semi-circle
Or curve of a sickle

From where they speak or gaze
Without mouths or eyes,

Inviting us to complete
The missing features. Their state

Lasts for millennia:
Even the cruder, tinier

Shapes are ever poised
To blink or to give voice

Notes

'Among the Volga Rus, AD 921'
The material derives from the account of Ahmad bin Fudhlan, translated in 'A Scandinavian cremation-ceremony', *Antiquity* 8 (1934) 58–62. The poem first appeared in 2000.

'The Euthanasiast'
The material derives from Michael Burleigh's sobering book, *Death and Deliverance*.

'To Louis Aragon, Et Al.'
The second quatrain alludes to Lenin's definition of politics as 'Who whom.'

'A White Officer in 1945'
Kolchak, Wrangel, and Denikin: generals in the defeated White armies in the Russian Civil War.

'A Veteran of the Terror'
The poem is based on the life of Nicolas Guénot (1754–1832), as related in Richard Cobb, *Reactions to the French Revolution*.

'XX'
The material derives from *The Double-Cross System* by J.C. Masterman, who set it up.

'Angleton's Names'
Culled from Robin Winks, *Cloak and Gown*.

'With Signs Following'
The picture appears in Thomas Burton, *Serpent-Handling Believers*.

'Shreds and Patches'
I did later find the syndrome described in *The Guardian* (1999) with reference to Shakespeare's Poor Tom.

'Solitude'
'Solitude' is by the Greek poet Kostis Palamas (1859–1943), sometimes the bombastic poet of the nation, sometimes terse as here.

'Homeward, Late …'
'Homeward, Late …' is by Tellos Agras (1899–1944), a Greek Laforguian – and more.

'Marche funèbre et perpendiculaire'
A Greek civil servant, K. G. Karyotakis (1896–1928) took his own life in the provincial town of Preveza after completing *Elegies and Satires* (1927), the longest suicide-note in Greek poetry.

'Homage to Johannes Bobrowski'
The last line quotes his poem 'Village Music', as translated by Ruth and Matthew Mead.

'Cantata for Anton Webern'
The composer wrote under four hours of music, including his well-known early piece, 'Im Sommerwind'; he was killed by an American serviceman in 1945.

'For William Lawes'
The musician, who had published no music in his lifetime, fell at the siege of Chester; line 3 takes a phrase from Thomas Fuller, *The Worthies of England*.

'The Ships'
This sample of *poésie pure* from 1920 is by the Greek poet Konstantinos Chatzopoulos (1868–1920).

'The Studio'
This distils a short memoir of the poet Lefteris Alexiou (1890–1964) by his son Stylianos.

'Still-Life with Musical Instruments'
The poem is based on one of several paintings of that name by Evaristo Basquenis (1617–1677) (Barber Institute, Birmingham).

'Mr Eliot's Confession'
The quotation is adapted from Bridget Cherry and Nikolaus Pevsner, *The Buildings of England. London 4: North*.

'Après le déluge'
Nasos Vayenas (1945–) is the doyen of Greek poet-critics. This version, along with others by this and other hands, appeared in *The Perfect Order: selected poems 1974–2010* (Anvil 2010).

Afterword
by A. E. Stallings

It seems astonishing that this is David Ricks's first full-length collection of poems, but then he has been in no haste, writing and polishing and storing up these gems over decades, even as he has laboured more publicly as a scholar of modern Greek literature. The result is a debut worth waiting for: formally adept, beautifully achieved poems that exist outside of the fluctuations of fashion, unabashedly serious, learned, and well crafted. As with Cavafy, a poet-historian whose poems are timeful rather than timeless, for Ricks, juxtaposition and irony are tools as useful as rhyme, rhythm, or register.

These poems exist on a kind of Cartesian chart where the axis of precise language intersects with human history. Ricks wields words knowing their real-world consequences. Language proves a driver of history, not just a casualty, as in this acerbic six liner:

> 'Ethnic Cleansing'
>
> The arguments remained specious.
> Meanwhile things followed the atrocious
>
> Imperative. The century
> Had done away with sanctuary.
>
> Populations fell into the chasm
> Opened by each neologism.

In couplets where rhymes are slippery and slant and enjambments slice across syntax, atrocities follow atrocious imperatives, whole populations fall into the chasm that opens between sanctuary and neologism. As we watch or read the news, probably more on social media now than anywhere else, wherein again whole populations are dismissed with dehumanizing terms, we realize how words are often the cobbles whereby roads to hell are paved.

Ricks has an eye for the illuminating anecdote that sheds light not only on its own moment but our own. Consider the close of the sonnet

'A White Officer in 1945' about a cavalry officer of the White Army in exile from Russia, who thinks back on

> Those starving botanists of Leningrad
> (Though he can't bear to call it by that name)
> Who would not eat their inventoried seeds

'Inventoried,' by taking up four syllables and two feet of valuable metrical real estate has the feeling of eking out, enumerating, and hanging on. Ricks also has a surgical touch with word choice: In 'A Veteran of the Terror' (we slowly realize it might be an aged tree being addressed that has survived from Revolutionary times) he performs a small miracle with the adjective 'deciduous', applied not to foliage but human heads.

There are poems on delightfully unlikely subjects, such as the nicknames of the CIA spymaster James Jesus Angleton: 'Mother', 'Orchid', 'Fisherman', 'Virginia Slim', 'Cadaver', 'Old Man', 'Poet'. As the last moniker suggests, it isn't as odd a topic for a series of poems as might first appear: Angleton was deeply interested in poetry, edited the student literary journal at Yale, and corresponded with Eliot and Pound. Is not spying as well as poetry an 'escape from personality', 'a wilderness of mirrors'? Ricks's playfulness with language is on display here: when Angleton names an orchid or two after his wife, he quips, 'there's classified for you'. But there is also a melancholy that reminds me a bit of the American poet Weldon Kees. We are left with a five-faceted portrait of an unknowable man, and yet a meditation also on the distilled counter-intelligence of being a poet. As Ricks points out:

> ... Just once,
> A poem of his got clipped in error to a report.
> Almost a definition of the poet, this:
> 'He can remember his own lies.'

Ricks's long engagement with modern Greek literature enriches these pages, not only in the several fine translations from Greek here – of Kostis Palamas, Nasos Vayenas, and the rarely translated Tellos Agras, as well as a new translation of Cavafy – but in poems about Cavafy ('Cavafy's Stationery') and a version from Karyotakis, the doomed youthful genius of Greek letters. (Imagine Keats if he were also a suicide.) With new Cavafy translations, one sometimes feels it is just moving deck chairs around, but in Ricks's splendid version of 'Sculptor from Tyana', Ricks is both bold in his Englishing ('You'll have heard I'm no tyro', he begins) and alive to the sound effects in the Greek, capturing its ad hoc rhymes with seemingly no effort. It's a dramatic monologue that owes something to Browning: indeed, the sculptor appears to be an ancient version of Claus of Innsbruck, casting Neptune's bronze sea horses. As readers, though, we are the potential buyer taking a tour about the shop and being led to the erotically ephebe head of Mercury. It is tantalizing to think what Ricks would do with more Cavafy poems.

But even in references to Greek writers, Ricks has a European sweep to his range of references, such as the five-part poem on the various abodes of Ugo Foscolo in England. Foscolo, an Italian poet and revolutionary, born in Zakynthos of a Greek mother, ended his days in England, penniless. In the section, 'Digamma Cottage', Ricks writes:

> So here he seized
> On a lost letter
> Posting it
> At his door:
> A slanted *F*.

Digamma – that slanted *F* – is an ancient letter of the Greek alphabet that stood for a 'w' (double-u) sound. It is moving to think of this erudite half-Greek Italian seizing on something lost and arcane even to Homeric Greek for the name of his cottage in exile, and which, in English, just looks like a wonky 'F' – 'posted', no less, as if a letter to the world, and seeming to stand, perhaps for failure rather than welcome.

Ricks is interested in what happens to painters, philosophers, and poets caught up in the meshing gears of events but is never glib or facile. Artists are not always victims. And in that case, how are we, the listeners and the beholders, implicated? Of the pro-Nazi expressionist Emil Nolde, Ricks writes:

> Forgive
>
> us if we turn from the
> giants and dancing
> girls and from anything that even
>
> reminds us of the human.

All of Ricks's poems, of course, very much remind us of the human. Even those most abstracted of human shapes, the mysterious Cycladic figures, anthropomorphize, in a slender sonnet of stacked couplets with delicate half rhymes that tease out their features:

> Without mouths or eyes,
>
> Inviting us to complete
> The missing features. Their state
>
> Lasts for millennia:
> Even the cruder, tinier
>
> Shapes are ever poised
> To blink or to give voice.

This is a poetry of close observation and fine-tuned ear, of sympathy even with art and human activity removed from us by a distance of millennia. Ricks's poetry, humane, intelligent, witty, precise, yet unpretentious, invites us in, to contemplate our responsibility to language, and to beware the ugly neologisms that enable us to abstract and make featureless the humanity of others.

Two Rivers Press has been publishing in and about Reading
since 1994. Founded by the artist Peter Hay (1951–2003),
the press continues to delight readers, local and further afield,
with its varied list of individually designed,
thought-provoking books.